51 LESSONS
That Cancer Taught Me

**My Unique Cancer Survivor Story of Faith,
Mindset, Spirit Even A Blue-Eyed Wolf**

RUSS SILLS

Published by Hemingway Publishers

Cover design by Hemingway Publishers

ISBN: Printed in the United States

Table of Contents

Introduction

In choosing to do this a little differently and in my own way, I have added relational inspiration quotes at the beginning of each chapter. I hope that you enjoy them.

Inspiration

"Never let success get to your head. Never let failure get to your heart."

"No matter what has happened to you in the past or what challenges you are facing now, walk in faith with God."

"Prayer is man's greatest power."

– W. Clement Stone

"I am strong because I have been weak, fearless because I have been afraid, wise because I have been foolish."

– Daily Inspirational Quotes

I am sure that you are wondering what a Blue-Eyed Wolf has to do with my cancer battle. For the longest time, I did not know myself. Although the wolf kept showing up in my dreams and it had a calming effect on me. So, was it just a recurring dream, or did it mean something? I needed all the help that I could get in my battle. It just seemed to be surgery after surgery. I did know that something was missing in my battle, and I wanted to see if the wolf represented anything in my current situation. I had to find out what. The most beautiful thing is that in that process, I found Spiritual reflection in that search, found out how it came into play, and the role that it played in my recovery.

My battle with cancer took me to some incredibly unique places, and I felt that sharing this story could be meaningful. More importantly, in the final section of this book, I shared the lessons that I learned from fighting cancer. There were many of them and I believe they are worth sharing. If even one life is saved because of them, then I will consider the time and effort that went into writing this book to be worth it.

I think it is important to say that I am not a physician or scientist, and I am not going to throw a bunch of credentials at you. In this book, I share my own personal experience and everything that I have learned and studied to understand how to fight cancer. I do believe that I am here thanks to the power of God, the power of prayer, awesome family support, great medical care and a crash course on the mind/body relationship. I also learned a lot about the internal power that we have over our experiences and emotions. Most importantly, I learned that this is a three-dimensional fight: mind, body, and spirit.

"I don't like all these scars, but it means that I was tougher than what tried to hurt me."

"Looking at my scars now reminds me that I am lucky to be alive."

"Sometimes the scars that you can't see are the hardest to heal."

– M. Hodkin

"Don't waste time underestimating yourself, dream big. Life was never meant to be safe; it was meant to be lived right up to the end."

– Caroline Myss

I was diagnosed with cancer at 62 years old—it was Head and Neck Cancer, Squamous Cell Carcinoma, Stage 4. I think one of the most devastating things you can hear from a doctor is the "C" word, especially when you've been healthy most of your life, stayed in fairly good shape, and never smoked or drank (okay, a couple of beers a month with a good meal is probably my max).

Being told you have cancer really rocks your world—it sure did mine. Statistics show that 92% of people who get head and neck cancer are smokers or tobacco users. I never was. That puts me in the 8% category of people who all wonder how they ended up with this horrible disease.

At this point, my journey has taken me through 25 surgeries (one and done would have been nice). Among them was a 26-plus-hour surgery that I never woke up from, which eventually put me into a 16-day coma—a near-death experience. It was during this time that I finally started hearing from God. During the journey, I've had numerous setbacks—even at the Mayo Clinic.

This journey also took me to a six-week stay at the Hope Lodge in Rochester, sponsored by the American Cancer Society. The Hope Lodge is where my heart truly broke. It was filled with children fighting cancer, and I lived alongside those children and their parents for about six weeks. I share some of my experiences with those brave kids in the chapter titled *"Oh, The Children."*

Then, the road took me to hyperbaric treatment and one of the largest oxygen therapy rooms in the world. That was a great experience. The next stop (oh so unique) was leech therapy. Yes—leeches!—Those little bloodsuckers found in rivers and lakes across the world. The leeches attach to an injured area to increase blood flow, and the Mayo Clinic was newly experimenting with this technique. I was part of the first group of patients they tried the new leech therapy on.

Although in my case, the leeches had to attach to the roof of my mouth (are you gagging yet?). Well, the worst that can happen is that you swallow a leech—and guess what? Yes, an intern managed to drop one down my throat. Yum.

What transpired next was totally amazing. You'll have to read the chapter *"That Sucks,"* appropriately named after those little creatures. I can laugh about it now, but it definitely wasn't funny at the time.

The last leg of my journey led me to Dr. Samir Mardini. He is an extremely famous and talented surgeon, and I was incredibly thankful to have him. He performed Mayo Clinic's first facial transplant, and he is now my surgeon. How I came to be under his care is also documented in this book.

I am so thankful for Dr. Mardini. What he has accomplished so far is truly amazing, and I believe he was heaven-sent.

Dedications

Gina Sills

I would like to dedicate this book to my beautiful wife, Gina. She is simply an awesome person inside and out. She even encouraged me to write this book. I could not be more blessed, and I thank God for her daily. Her beauty and attitude just light up a room when she enters. Her inner spiritual beauty is reflected in her face and her heart. She is my wife and my best friend. She has been beside me every step of the way in this cancer battle. She is a dedicated wife, mother, grandmother, and nurse. Her story is simply amazing. She came from the humblest beginning. At the age of 5, she had lost both parents. Her father had decided to run out on a beautiful wife and three of the cutest little girls. Then, her mother was killed in an automobile accident not more than two miles from home. Thank God for a special grandmother who took on raising all 3 girls despite being poor herself. There was obviously a lot of love in that family. Thank you, Grandma, for your sacrifice. Also, a special thank you to Gina's older sisters, Robin Oswald and Roxanne Outt, who always took Gina under their wing and helped teach her as a kid. Lots of love, truly little money, these girls were so poor that their hand-me-down clothes came from boys. Gina has never forgotten how poor they were and where she came from. That is another part of her beauty.

Gina loved school, but after losing Grandma, she dropped out of high school in her early teenage years. Life for her and her sisters back then was tough, especially after losing Grandma. Gina got married young and became pregnant. She was a child raising a child. Gina never gave up on her dreams of finishing school and becoming a nurse. She eventually finished high school and got accepted into a nursing program at Crowder College. She worked her behind off, working a full-time job while raising kids and working on her nursing degree all at the same time. Gina finally graduated from college, got her RN certification, and started her nursing career. A few years later, she got her BSN at Wesleyan University. Wow, she is an impressive, hard-working lady. She never gave up her dream and got there through hard work and dedication. She's an awesome story herself. I love her more than words can say. Gina, if you look in my eyes, you will see me. If you look in my heart, you will see you.

Gina, as you look in the mirror, I hope you see what I see—you are beautiful. Thanks for always being there.

David Brewer

I lost my nephew a couple of years ago. He and his wife were taking a motorcycle trip, and a car pulled right out in front of them. David had an awesome wife named Stacie, and we lost them both that day. He was a police officer in the Joplin Police Force. That is all he ever wanted to be; a police officer. He was a good one, according to his Chief and everyone he worked with. He was honest, fair, had a huge heart, and was someone who always ran into danger as opposed to the other direction. He was someone who always had your back.

There are a couple of ironic things about the way David died. First, he had spent his whole life on motorcycles since the age of seven, when he started riding motocross. The second is that he was a motorcycle officer and rode one almost daily. We were all shocked to lose David that way.

At his funeral, police officers from several surrounding states came to honor him. There were even officers from as far away as North Carolina who came to pay their respects, and the funeral procession stretched for miles. It was one of the most impressive honors I've ever had the opportunity to be part of. Those police officers truly are a band of brothers. We lost a hero that day.

Chapter 1
The Tale of Two Wolves
and the Power of Mindset

Inspiration

"Positive thinking is a valuable tool that can help you overcome obstacles, deal with pain and reach new goals."

– Amy Morin

"Your mind is a powerful thing. When you fill it with positive thoughts, your life will start to change."

"Don't waste your time in anger, regret, worries or grudges. They all can affect healing."

"The soul always knows what to do to heal itself. The challenge is to silence the mind."

– Caroline Myss

No matter who you are or where you come from, you have probably faced several challenges in your life. Encountering challenges is a natural part of life that unites us all here on earth. Whether you're in the middle of a major life challenge right now or possibly preparing for one in the future, there's nothing wrong with needing inspirational thoughts to help you through tough times.

Sometimes, hearing an uplifting story can get you the motivation that you need. The story of the *"Tale of Two Wolves"* is a parable in the Native American tradition that has been passed down through generations. Hopefully, hearing this story again will empower you to change your mindset and approach life with a more positive and productive outlook.

In the story, an Old Cherokee is teaching his grandson about life. "A fight is going on inside me, and it is a fight between two wolves. One is evil—he is anger, envy, sorrow, regret, greed, arrogance, self-pity, guilt, resentment, inferiority, lies, false pride, ego, and superiority."

He continued, "The other is good—he is joy, peace, love, hope, serenity, humility, kindness, empathy, generosity, truth, compassion, and faith." The same fight is going on in each of us.

The grandson thought about what he had just heard his grandfather say, then asked the grandfather, "Which wolf will win?"

The old Cherokee replied, "The one you feed."

Whether this is the first time you've heard this story or you've heard it many times before, it serves as an important reminder of the power we have over our experiences and emotions.

As I look back over my extensive battle, I ask myself: how was I controlling my experiences and emotions? Was I feeding both wolves? Probably so.

Are you feeling sorry for yourself? It is too easy to feel like a victim when we encounter challenging situations in our lives. We try to understand both the negative and the positive. But too often, on the negative side, we end up feeling sorry for ourselves and placing blame on others.

We look around and try to make sense of what's happening. Is it our way of coping? Is it our way of trying to understand—and mentally control—the uncontrollable?

In our attempt to feel more in control by feeling sorry for ourselves or even possibly blaming others, we end up removing our own power. As we assign blame and become more dependent on other people, we give up control. The more we depend on others, the less control we have over the situation.

Think about it for a minute: the moment we become dependent on certain people or certain things to make us feel a certain way, which wolf are we feeding?

When you're no longer taking responsibility for your emotions, which wolf are you feeding? When you stop taking responsibility for your experiences, which wolf are you feeding? When you fall into self-pity or feel sorry for yourself, which wolf are you feeding?

It's important to understand that emotions such as sorrow, regret, resentment, and inferiority all lie at the feet of the evil wolf. Do you feed the evil wolf, the one that says you're a failure, that no one will love or understand you? This wolf represents your depression, your anxiety, your self-doubt, and your damaged self-esteem. Are you feeding this wolf?

Or are you feeding the good wolf, the one filled with joy, peace, love, hope, serenity, kindness, empathy, generosity, truth, compassion, and faith?

As you fight diseases like cancer, you need to feed the good wolf because healing begins within. Conquering negative thoughts and emotions is huge. It plays an extremely important role in your fight against cancer.

The message here is that you have more power over your healing and happiness than you think you do. You will find yourself battling conflicting emotions many times throughout your life. It's important to recognize those conflicting feelings within you and choose to feed the values that matter most.

The more you focus on the positive emotions inside you, the less room there is for the negative ones. Over time, you'll begin facing life's difficulties with greater confidence and peace of mind.

Mindset is a key theme in this story. Your mindset not only has a powerful effect on your outlook on life but also on your healing. You can't beat cancer simply by thinking it away, but your mindset can influence the health of your body and strengthen your fight against cancer. It can play a huge role in your recovery.

I used the mind-body relationship as part of my personal battle. Hopefully, some of you will, too.

Mindset

If you think that you are beaten, you are.

If you think that you dare not, you don't.

If you like to win but think you can't,

It is almost a cinch that you won't.

If you think that you will lose, you've lost.

For out in this world, we find,

Success begins with a person's will.

It is all in the state of mind.

If you think that you are outclassed, you are.

You have to think high to rise.

You have to be sure of yourself before

You can ever win the prize.

Life's battles don't always go,

To the stronger or faster man

But sooner or later, the person who wins,

Is the one who thinks he can.

Walter D. Wintle (poet)

Chapter 2
Connection Between Mind, Body and Health

<u>Inspiration</u>

"Positive thinking has the power to turn a hard day into a manageable one and a good day into an even better one."

"90% of the battle is getting yourself in the right state of mind."

– Chuck Swindoll

"The spiritual journey is the unlearning of fear and the acceptance of love."

– Marianne Williamson

Definition – Mindset is the driving force in the quest for success and achievement.

"Fear defeats more people than any other one thing in the world."

– Ralph Waldo Emerson.

"The mindset that you choose will help you win or lose."

– LeAura Alderson

I have given up on the need to know why things happen as they do. I will never know, and constant wondering is constant suffering. Constant suffering hinders healing. Besides, only God knows, and I am sure that is a question that will be commonly asked when we meet God.

We all have the power of the will to live, but this power is stronger in some people than in others. Just look at the power of some of our wounded warrior veterans. Wow, talk about the will to live.

Today, many physicians have seen how similar patients with the same diagnosis and the same degree of illness experience vastly different results. It has caused some physicians to look more closely at the mind when it comes to healing and the will to live. Of course, the biology of cancer, the type of cancer, and how far along the cancer is, will, in some cases, dictate the course—regardless of a patient's attitude and fighting spirit.

But there are also patients with faith and positive attitudes who are better able to cope with cancer problems, and they tend to respond better to therapy. One of the apparent differences between these two kinds is that one patient is optimistic, while the other is pessimistic.

Recognizing the wisdom that physical and psychological elements are not separate, I believe them to be vitally linked parts of the entire system. I believe that there is a correlation between mind, body, and health—Call it the whole. A part can never be well unless the whole is well. Recognize this wisdom that the physical and psychological elements are not separate.

Here is what I see as the *"whole healing system"*: Physical, emotional, psychological, nutritional, and exercise-based components. There are several important things to consider when you are trying to heal from cancer.

Some doctors and researchers are now experimenting with actively engaging the mind in the body's combat against cancer. They now believe that mental and emotional activity can play a significant role in a person's recovery. There are a few doctors and psychologists who believe that the proper attitude may have a direct effect on cell function. Personally, I believe that mental and emotional activity can indeed play a major role in recovery.

I start every day with a prayer, and in that prayer, I ask God to help me keep focused on a positive mindset. I don't know exactly how much of a role my mindset played, but I firmly believe that it contributed to my recovery. If I had to face it again, I would attack it the same way. I believe the mindset you choose can help you win— or lose.

Some doctors are now using visualization and biofeedback to create positive images of what is occurring in a person's body. We do know that both techniques are helpful as they encourage positive thinking and promote relaxation in the healing process. However, this must only be done in addition to conventional therapy. I am curious to see what long-term results these methods may produce.

How much control the mind has on the immune system is still unknown. But consider me one of the people who believes that positive thinking and an increase in the will to live can have a positive effect on the healing process.

Today, more doctors acknowledge that the mind impacts the body. That connection is now becoming accepted in mainstream science. Several clinical studies on the heart have shown that stress reduction can reduce plaque and lower the risk of heart attacks. They are finding comparable results in studies of other diseases. Think about it—when you get angry because someone is annoying you, you can feel your blood pressure rise. Or when you're scared, your heart starts racing. Your body responds instantly. There is a connection between the mind and the body. So, it makes sense that feelings and emotions can have a long-term impact on our health. I believe that emotions can affect other parts of the body—including the body's ability to fight cancer.

Where does fear fall in all of this?

Fear does not stop death—but it can rob you of true living. It can paralyze your spirit before it ever touches your body. Which begs the question: How can emotional fear hurt your healing? Fear is a powerful emotion that can affect your physical condition—and especially hinder healing.

Never allow fear to dictate your decisions. Choosing fear in the face of adversity doesn't just affect you—it affects the people around you, too.

What if you replaced fear with faith? Many times in life, you may have to choose between the two. Choose wisely—make the right choice according to God's will.

Being free of fear doesn't mean you will never feel afraid; it means you don't let fear influence your decisions. It also means you don't let fear control you. True courage comes from acting in spite of fear, not in the absence of it. Fear must be confronted by doing the very thing that makes you afraid.

Basically, there are two paths you can walk—faith or fear. What if faith were your natural reaction to threats and challenges? Can you imagine going one day without worrying about failure, rejection, or distress? In *Matthew 8:26,* Jesus asks, "Why are you afraid?"

The most repeated command in the Bible is "Do not be afraid." God is greater than any fear you will encounter, and He is with you always.

"Fear has two meanings—Forget Everything and Run or Face Everything and Rise."

– Zig Ziglar.

Fear exists nowhere but in your mind. And while it may never fully disappear, it will always try to return—knocking on the door of your heart and mind. Do not let fear influence you. Conquer it by taking one step at a time.

One step forward is still forward, and God honors progress over perfection. Never underestimate the power of little victories.

When a father is walking his 4-year-old child down a busy street or through a crowded mall, he reaches out and says, "Hold on to my hand." When fear begins to overcome your faith, remember that it is exactly when it's time to reach out and hold your Heavenly Father's hand.

Fear is persistent and will try to become a constant part of your journey. It will attempt to steal your thoughts, your peace, and your emotions. Resist it. Hand it over to your Heavenly Father.

To heal your body, you must also heal your mind. A whole heart starts with a whole mindset.

Here are ways to heal your mind:

- Believe you can win. Believe you can get well.
- Fight fear with faith.
- Keep your thoughts positive.
- Forget the past.
- Forgive people—including yourself.
- Pray.

Chapter 3
Strength - Physical, Mental and Spiritual

<u>Inspiration</u>

"All things are possible to he who believes"

– Mark 9:23

"Sometimes we struggle to understand just how much we depend on God. We don't see or hear Him, so we perceive Him as distant. God not only created us, but He also sustains us."

"Success is converting weakness into strength."

– Zig Ziglar

"You never know how strong you are until being strong is the only choice you have"

– Bob Marley

"Be on guard against self-pity when you are sick or weary. This trap is one of the greatest dangers that you face."

Battling your cancer and the trauma that comes with it will require your physical, mental, and spiritual strength. Remember that stress takes a toll on your body and affects your healing.

Your physical strength plays a role in almost everything you do. The better your physical condition, the better equipped you are to fight the health challenges that come your way. With physical strength, your ability to fight disease is stronger, and you can recover more quickly when you do get sick. Additionally, it is less likely that stress and worry will slow you down. Remember, the struggle you are in today develops the strength you'll need for tomorrow.

Controlling your mind is huge. Dealing with the many disappointments and challenges of life requires mental strength. Mental strength helps control your emotions. Without mental strength, your emotions easily head toward fear and doubt. Without strength of mind, your emotions can control you. Mental toughness helps maintain a sharp mind under the challenges and pressures that you will face. Mental toughness helps you remain focused on what is important.

Spiritual strength is what we receive from God in grace. Spirituality is an awareness of God's presence within us. God is your refuge and strength, an ever-present help in your times of trouble. Prayer is your greatest weapon. It is a spiritual medicine. The stronger your spiritual strength, the stronger your mind and body will be.

Chapter 4
Cancer Changed Me

Inspiration

"I can do all things through Christ which strengthens me."

– Philippians 4-13

"Everything that you ever wanted is sitting on the other side of fear."

– George Addair

"Our lives change externally as we change internally."

– Caroline Myss

"There are times to fight and times to surrender. When I speak of surrender, here is what I mean. Surrender your hate, your pride, your ego, your jealousy, your need to be right, your grudges, your guilt, your shame, your resentment, and your sin."

No one wants to hear the words *"You have cancer,"* yet each year, almost two million people in the United States alone do. While cancer is one of the worst things that can happen to you, God has a way of strengthening you and teaching you through the battle. Cancer will change you—and hopefully, for the better.

Cancer changed me. It made me a better person. It reset my perspective on many things. It taught me how precious life truly is and reminded me to be thankful for every single day. It humbled me. It taught me the importance of love—it made me love deeper and taught me to say "I love you" more. It taught me to value family more. It also taught me to value my friends more.

I learned to acknowledge people more. I shake more hands. I give more hugs. It taught me how to live with intention and purpose. It taught me to forgive—I still struggle with this sometimes, but God knows I'm working on it.

It all reminds me of that Tim McGraw song, *"Live Like You Were Dying."*

While I carry many regrets from this battle—and yes, it has been full of pain and suffering—I can still look back with a small smile. Because I know this journey shaped who I am today: a stronger, better, and more caring person.

And I can assure you—I'm not going back to yesterday.

I was a different person then.

My Story Begins

Chapter 5
The Sore

Inspiration

"Being a believer in Christ does not make you immune to sickness, hardship, or challenges."

"Being a believer in Christ does mean that you have an anchor to hold on to during the storm."

"There is no such thing as a problem-free life. Everybody in the Bible had their challenges, and you will too."

"My faith didn't remove the pain, but it helped me get through it."

A little personal history: My professional journey began with a solid foundation in Telecommunications Engineering, backed by degrees in Computer Science and Management. During my younger years, I served a six-year term in the Air Force, a time that was both challenging and rewarding. While I cherished the discipline, camaraderie, and experiences I gained in the military, I had a deep desire to expand my horizons and apply my education in a civilian career.

I was fortunate to have the opportunity to begin this new chapter at NASA's Jet Propulsion Laboratory (JPL) in Pasadena, California.

It was a prestigious and exciting role, especially since it was with NASA—a name that commanded respect. Though I started at the bottom of the totem pole, I was drawn to the incredible possibilities the job offered. The work was fascinating, and I had the privilege of supporting telecommunications for several high-profile deep space programs, including Mercury, Pioneer, Voyager, SeaSat, and Helios.

One of the most thrilling aspects of that role was getting the chance to see the Space Shuttle Columbia up close before it even launched. The energy around that project was electric, and I knew I was part of something groundbreaking.

However, life had other plans. A devastating blow struck when I lost my wife in an automobile accident while living in California. The weight of this loss was profound, and the grief left me feeling disconnected from my surroundings. I realized I couldn't stay in California, a place filled with so many memories. I needed a change— a fresh start—and I found it when a good friend who once worked at NASA reached out to me. He had since moved to a management position at GTE and offered me a financial opportunity I couldn't turn down. It was a chance to rebuild, both professionally and personally.

So, I packed up and moved on. GTE eventually became Verizon, and I spent several fulfilling years there, learning, growing, and contributing to the evolution of the telecommunications industry. But as I continued to grow, I felt the pull of a different direction—one that aligned more with my evolving interests and values.

Most of the remainder of my career was spent in the healthcare industry, a sector I found to be both challenging and immensely rewarding. I took on a leadership role as the Director of Network Services and Telecommunications for Catholic Health Initiatives, where I was responsible for overseeing technology infrastructure across 15 hospitals. This role not only deepened my technical expertise but also gave me the satisfaction of knowing that the work we did had a direct impact on patient care and the healthcare system at large. It was here that I truly felt I had found my niche, contributing to an industry that changed lives every day.

Looking back, I realize how each chapter in my career has been a stepping stone—each one leading me to new opportunities and helping shape me into the person I am today. Every experience, whether at NASA, GTE, or in healthcare, has added a unique layer to my career, pushing me to expand my capabilities and enrich my understanding of the world. It's been a journey of growth, resilience, and learning, one that continues to evolve as I move forward.

Eventually, the organization decided to outsource its entire network, which impacted more than 75 hospitals nationwide. Along with a large group of talented colleagues, I was laid off. I had just turned 62 and, after decades of hard work, was hoping to peacefully finish the final chapter of my career and transition into retirement.

Not long after, I found a new opportunity with NPC International (National Pizza Company), the largest Pizza Hut franchise in the United States at the time, operating between 1,300 and 1,400 locations nationwide. They hired me to manage telecommunications for the entire company. It was a wonderful job, with great people, and I saw it as a positive shift in my career after a long and meaningful journey.

One afternoon, while on a lunch break, I noticed a sore in my mouth. It was located on the gum line behind one of my molars. At first, I didn't think much of it and tried a few over-the-counter products to treat it. However, the pain didn't go away, and the sore seemed to worsen. My initial thought was that it must be a bad tooth.

I decided to take the rest of the day off and went to the dentist. He took some X-rays and examined the area around the sore, ultimately concluding that the tooth next to it needed to be extracted. After administering Novocain, we proceeded with the extraction.

However, a few days later, I noticed something alarming: a black secretion was oozing from the opening where the tooth had been removed. It wasn't blood—it was black, and it seemed to be spreading across the area. It didn't feel right. It didn't look right.

Panicked, I immediately returned to the dentist. "What's going on?" I asked him, desperate for answers. He was just as puzzled, offering only theories without any clear explanation. He referred me to an oral surgeon, but his diagnosis was similarly inconclusive.

Frustrated and concerned, I decided to seek the help of a real doctor.

My next stop was Dr. McDonald, an ENT specialist at Mercy in Joplin. Dr. McDonald was a remarkable physician, one of the hardest-working doctors I had ever met. On any given day, he could see up to 45 patients. My daughter had worked for him, and she was always in awe of his dedication and professionalism. Mercy lost a great doctor when he left.

Fortunately, I had made the right choice by coming to him.

Dr. McDonald quickly examined the area around the sore and the black secretion. After some deliberation, he told me he suspected the issue was a form of skin cancer called Squamous Cell Carcinoma. To confirm the diagnosis, he took a biopsy and rushed it to the lab for testing.

When the results came back, Dr. McDonald's suspicions were confirmed. It was indeed Squamous Cell Carcinoma, a diagnosis that, while difficult to hear, gave me the clarity I had been searching for.

Chapter 6
So Now We Know

Inspiration

"Trust in the lord with all your heart and do not lean on your own understanding."

- Proverbs 3:5.

"Never let a bad situation bring out the worst in you. Stay positive and be the strong person that God created you to be."

"God's strength and power show themselves the most in your weakest times."

"Courage combined with faith is a strong combination. Don't be afraid to take a chance. "

When I received the call to return and discuss the diagnosis with Dr. McDonald, I knew right then that we were dealing with something serious. If it hadn't been, he could have just told me over the phone. As I mentioned earlier, there are very few things that "sucker punch" you as hard as hearing the word *cancer*.

Dr. McDonald was incredible in how he handled the moment. He took time to explain what I might expect next and also spoke with me about the mental battle ahead—something just as important as the physical fight when facing this horrible disease.

Dr. McDonald had already contacted Dr. Pinheiro at Mercy Springfield. Dr. Pinheiro, an ENT specialist, was one of the best in this part of the country. Dr. McDonald wanted to make sure I was on his list. Thank you again, Dr. McDonald— Mercy lost a great one when you left.

Dr. Pinheiro was the next stop. We were scrambling to get on his schedule because the black mass— Squamous Cell Carcinoma (I will use the term SCC going forward)— was spreading at an alarming rate. SCC was now spreading over the roof of my mouth, and the speed at which it was doing so was alarming. I was totally surprised at how fast it could spread once it hit the air. Really scary stuff right there.

Dr. Pinheiro got me on the surgical scheduled quickly. Pinheiro was going to do the cancer removal, and a second surgeon—whom I'll call Dr. J —was in charge of reconstruction. I will call him Dr. J, as the last thing that I want to do is paint someone in a negative light. I have been lucky to have had some outstanding professionals throughout this journey. So now, the first surgery was set. My post-surgery cancer treatment was going to take place at C. H. (Chub) O'Reilly Cancer Center in Springfield. Have you heard of Chub? He and his father (C. F.) founded O'Reilly Auto Parts Stores.

Chapter 7
Faith and Prayer

<u>Inspiration</u>

"In my deepest, darkness moments. It was prayer that got me through it."

- Nelson Mandela

"Faith is believing in an awesome God when I am full of fear and uncertainty,"

"Faith is a strong confidence in God's grace, so certain that a person could stake his life on it."

- Martin Luther King

"In the wind, I found my breath. In the storm, I found my strength. Fighting cancer, I found my bravery. In all these, I found the courage to be myself."

- Author unknown

I come from a strong family of believers and churchgoers—including two ministers in my immediate family. As for myself, I've always had a strong belief in God, though I haven't always made the kind of church sacrifices I probably should have.

But when Sunday rolls around, if I am not physically in church, I'm usually reading the Bible or listening to preachers like Hagee, Carpenter, Prince, Jackson, Duplantis, Franklin, or Warren. I've read the Bible and even attended a Christian university, where I was required to take a Bible class. And when you take a class, you're tested on every chapter—so I've picked up some knowledge along the way.

But even so, there is so much more to the Bible than most people can fully grasp. There's also so much more to life—and to the afterlife—than we'll ever truly understand. And there is certainly more to what God expects from us than we often realize.

My wife is a believer, too, and there's quite a bit of prayer that happens under this roof. I begin every prayer by thanking God for His many blessings. I never asked for much through prayer—not until I was diagnosed with this horrible disease.

I know that God intends for each of us to go through both good times and bad. It's the tough times that challenge us, humble us, and ultimately draw us closer to Him. While this cancer diagnosis came as a complete surprise, I believe it's just one of the many challenges I was meant to endure.

The Bible says, *"God will not give us more than we can endure."* Sometimes I'm amazed at what I've already endured—but I also feel I've reached my threshold. At times, I can't help but think of that old Elvis song, *"This Time You Gave Me a Mountain."* It feels incredibly fitting for everything I've been through.

I truly believe that I wouldn't be here today without the power of prayer. Every day I'm still alive, I thank God. My wife, Gina, has so many wonderful friends and followers on Facebook. Every time I go in for another surgery, she asks her community to pray for us—and each time, more than 150 people join in prayerAnd that does not include prayer from the churches. Wow! Thank you to all the beautiful souls who've taken out time to pray for us. We love and appreciate every one of you.

I often wonder about non-believers — where do they turn when they're facing something like cancer? Or when they're dealing with heart problems, stroke, or diabetes? Or when their 3-year-old child is fighting for their life? Where do they turn their faith? Mankind?

Through all of this, I've never lost faith. I never stopped believing. I never asked "why," and I never looked for someone to blame — especially not God. I believe that a strong faith is key to healing. You'll read more about that in the "51 Lessons Learned" chapter.

Like most people in that 8% bracket who never smoked and tried to do things right, I have to wonder—where did this disease come from? I learned early in life that I didn't like tobacco smoke. My maternal grandparents were wonderful people who loved to travel. They visited all 48 mainland states, always by car. I would often go with them during summer breaks when I wasn't playing baseball (which I absolutely loved — I was always an All-Star and played all summer long).

The only downside of those road trips was that my grandfather smoked. He'd smoke in the car with the A/C on. Back then, cars had these little triangle windows called "wings," and I swear the only thing those were good for was flicking ashes outside. They didn't let much air out. Inside that car, your eyes would burn, your clothes and hair would reek of smoke, and sometimes it looked like a scene straight out of a Cheech and Chong movie — nothing but smoke everywhere. That entire generation seemed to smoke, and while I understand it now, it always struck me as a filthy habit. After those trips, I never had any interest in smoking.

Faith in hard times allows you to find peace in God's presence. He gives us faith so we may use it to recognize His work, even when we're surrounded by uncertainties. A great question to ask God in those moments is:

"Lord, what do You want me to learn from all of this?"

Chapter 8
Success and Failure

Inspiration

"Failure is the key to success. Each mistake teaches us something."

– M. Ueshiba

"More than that, we rejoice in our sufferings, knowing that suffering produces endurances, and endurance produces character and character produces hope"

– Romans 5:3-5

"You cannot choose what happens to you in life. But you can fight to help choose the outcome."

"Note to myself -take more chances in life. If you fail, keep trying."

I had a tough time writing this chapter because, through most of it, I was in a comatose state. It is now time for my first surgery, and looking back, all I can say is—wow. I had no idea what I was in for. This wasn't just a routine procedure—it turned into a marathon battle for my life.

Dr. Pinheiro, the skilled surgeon I trusted, had successfully completed the removal of the cancer. But once his part was done, it was Dr. J's turn to rebuild the palate. His job was to perform what they call a "flap procedure." This involves moving bone, skin, and veins—essentially transplanting living tissue from one part of the body to another. It's a delicate, complex dance where precision and timing are everything.

But something went wrong. I don't know the exact details because, by then, I was on the anesthesia end of things—lost to the darkness. What was supposed to be a 10-to-12-hour surgery turned into a 26-hour nightmare. They were still working on me, still trying to fix whatever had gone wrong. I was under anesthesia for so long that even when I finally recovered enough to wake up, it was only for a brief moment before I slipped back into a deep, unresponsive sleep.

Over 26 hours on the operating table, followed by a 16-day coma. That wasn't how it was supposed to go. What should have been a long but manageable surgery turned into a nightmare. When I finally woke up, it wasn't relief—it was confusion. I learned that my coma had been drug-induced. Gina, desperate to see me awake, had asked the doctors to stop all medications, and that's what finally brought me back.

But waking up was just the beginning of another battle. I was weak—unbelievably weak. I couldn't talk, couldn't eat. I was a shadow of the strong man who had gone in. And worse, Dr. J, the surgeon who was supposed to rebuild my palate, was gone—no explanation, no goodbye. Just gone.

I don't know why he left, and I won't paint anyone in a negative light, but the reality was harsh—I still needed help, and my body was barely hanging on. Time for some prayer. Because when everything else is stripped away, faith is all you have left.

Chapter 9
On to Radiation

Inspirational

"Faith is strength, when we feel that we have none."

- Catherine Pulsifer

"Faith is hope, when all else seems lost."

"If you have a good support system, like your family and friends, then you are blessed. Believe in God, believe in yourself and stay unwavering in your beliefs."

"May your heart be kind, your mind fierce and your spirit brave."

– Kate Forsyth

Radiation treatments should have started sooner, but because of the coma, they were delayed. If any cancer cells remained after the surgery, radiation was critical to kill the remaining cells. So, after the failed surgery and the coma, we were finally at a point where we could begin moving forward with the radiation process.

For those of you who've never experienced radiation treatments, here's what it's like: they create a custom plastic cast of your upper torso. Mine covered my head and face and extended all the way down to my waist and hip area. It fit so snugly that it captured the exact outline of my face, jaw, and nose.

The cast has built-in snaps, and once you're lying on the radiation table, the entire cast is placed over your face and torso and locked into place. You're completely immobilized—unable to move your upper body. Then, they position the radiation machine with precision, aligning it to the exact spot where the treatment is needed, and the process begins.

Being strapped down like that was difficult for me. I don't like being confined, and that's exactly what this plastic cast did—restrain me entirely. It took some time to get used to it. Wow!!

You hear the humming of the radiation machine, but of course, you feel nothing. My radiation was targeted directly at the cheekbone area on my right side. I can't recall exactly how long each treatment lasted, but it felt like I was in that radiation room for anywhere from an hour to 90 minutes a day. I do remember this much—I had 36 full-dose treatments. The dosage was higher, and there were extra sessions because of the earlier delays.

As for side effects, I don't recall many—except occasional dizziness when I first sat up and general fatigue. But it's hard to pinpoint how much of that tiredness was from the radiation alone. I choked easily, could barely swallow, and was being fed through a gastric tube in my stomach. Add to that the fact I was still recovering from a 16-day coma and had experienced rapid weight loss—all of that surely played a role in my exhaustion.

While I knew the radiation was helping kill off cancer cells, I had no idea what kind of collateral damage it was causing.

At Mayo, they take a lot of imaging—and it was during one of those scans that they found a hole in my right cheek, likely caused by repeated radiation in the same spot. The hole was larger than a quarter but smaller than a half-dollar. What we didn't know then was that this hole would become a major obstacle in my recovery. It would impact the contour of my face and create significant challenges when fitting a denture or obturator.

I also began to experience hearing loss and balance issues. I lost about 60% of the hearing in my right ear, and the proximity of the radiation gun to that ear likely made things worse.

At the time, my wife, Gina — a registered nurse—was working at the Mercy Springfield Campus. Since my treatments were daily, Mercy provided us with access to a nearby apartment located just behind the chapel. It was a blessing. We had a place to stay within walking distance of both Gina's department and the radiation center.

Thank you, Mercy, for the room. And thank you especially for placing it behind the chapel—I was able to stop in and pray before each treatment.

Chapter 10
My Time to Ring the Bell

Inspirational

"Above all else guard your heart, for everything that you do flows from it."

— Proverbs 4:23.

"Fall seven times and stand up eight"

— Japanese Proverb

"Approach your disease with a strong faith, optimism and a remarkable grace."

"Limits, like fear, are often an illusion."

— Michael Jordan

Thirty-six radiation treatments are a lot, and it felt never-ending. Plus, I was taking them right at Christmas and New Year's, which dragged the time out. I finally got to "ring the bell." This is a huge accomplishment for anyone fighting cancer. "Ringing the bell" is a merit badge (a sense of accomplishment)— especially when so many people die from this terrible disease. The goal is that both patients and staff will find it an uplifting and pleasant experience during an otherwise stressful journey.

When you ring the bell at Mercy, the radiation oncology staff members that can break free for a couple of minutes line up in the hallway to wish you a nice send-off. The whole team that was with me during my daily treatments was there. My wife, Gina, was also there, showing her dedication as always. It was a nice send-off after a long radiation journey.

Among the items I was dismissed with was the upper torso cast. I kept the upper torso cast and had it hanging up high in my garage. I have a love/hate relationship with the cast. There have been times when I just wanted to take it out and use it for target practice. Then, at other times, I remember it is a reminder of where I am and how hard I fought to be here. So, it is still hanging around.

Ringing the bell is a very emotional and meaningful part of a patient's recovery. It signifies an important milestone on their cancer journey, and it also signifies a celebratory moment. Tears, smiles, and hugs accompany this ceremony. Ringing the bell inspires hope, excitement, and a feeling of accomplishment.

I rang this bell for myself and for anyone who has ever fought this horrible disease. I rang this bell for the physicians, nurses and support staff who helped me in my battle with this horrible disease. I rang this bell for my wife, family and friends, who became part of my awesome support system. I rang this bell for anyone who offered up a prayer in my support. I rang this bell, Thanking God for His support.

Chapter 11
Chemo, Weakness and Weight Loss

Inspiration

"Weakness of attitude becomes weakness of character."

"Surgery weakens you; radiation wipes you out, and Chemo just piles on."

"Let your faith be bigger than your fears."

– Joyce Meyer

"Never lose hope, storms make people stronger and never last forever."

– Roy T Bennett

Dr. Snider was more than just my Oncologist in Springfield— she is another doctor that I am thankful for. She was a guardian in my fight for life. From the moment I was assigned to her, I felt a sense of reassurance and comfort that I would never forget. The special attention she gave to every detail of my care made all the difference. It wasn't just her medical expertise that stood out; it was her bedside manner that truly set her apart. She didn't just treat me as a patient; she saw me as a person, and that made all the difference. Her genuine interest in my well-being gave me the strength to fight each day, even when the journey seemed impossible.

As the time for chemotherapy approached, Dr. Snider's concern for me deepened. My weight loss and weakness had become more than just a physical issue— they were symptoms of something far greater. From the very beginning, she knew I was no longer the person I had once been. I was a shell of myself, and it pained her to see it.

Gina and I sat down with Snider to develop a plan that would be in my best interest. I don't know exactly what my weight was at the time, but I was still losing weight at a pace that terrified Gina. At that time, Eating was impossible—I survived on nutritional drinks fed through a gastric tube.

By the time we managed to turn things around, I had lost a staggering 80 pounds. At that rate, I can only imagine that Gina and my family feared that I was staring death in the face. To be honest, I had those thoughts too.

The weight fell off so fast that Dr. Snider insisted we bring in a nutritionist to get my strength back before even considering chemo. It was no longer just about treatment; it was about survival.

I've never had an addiction and can't begin to understand how hard it is to overcome one, but I can tell you this—having to quit eating for over two years was the toughest fight of my life. It was especially brutal during the holidays, when the house was full of incredible food and the warmth of family gatherings—when the scent of my wife's cooking filled the air, tempting me with meals I couldn't have.

Dr. Snider made sure that I had regular visits, each one more crucial than the last. She kept a watchful eye on every detail—my cancer, my strength, and my weight. She had a clear target in mind, a precise point where we would move forward with chemotherapy. It wasn't just about surviving; it was about making sure my body was strong enough to handle the intense treatment. After working closely with the nutrition staff for a couple of months, I began to improve in ways I hadn't expected. The weight loss finally stopped, and my strength began to come back, little by little, like the slow but steady return of light after a long, dark storm.

"Let's wait and see where we are in a couple of months," Dr. Snider said. So, we did just that.

As time passed, a quiet confidence started to grow. We reached a turning point—a moment where the fear that had once weighed so heavily on me began to lift. Dr. Snider, with her calm and steady approach, began to believe that chemotherapy might not be necessary after all. It was a hard decision, but she trusted her judgment. We kept the chemo on hold, but the watchful monitoring didn't stop. Every visit, every test, every careful observation ensured that we were leaving no stone unturned. Dr. Snider made sure we were getting it all, making sure it wasn't returning.

And then, there came the moment when we decided to move forward without chemo. The weight of that decision was enormous, but it was made with the trust that my body had regained the strength it needed. It was the right call, and though it was a decision grounded in hope, it felt right in my bones. If any signs of the cancer returned, we knew the chemo would be the next step. But, for now, the road ahead felt like one I could walk without that heavy burden looming over me.

Looking back, I am so thankful for that moment—thankful that we chose the path we did. It turned out to be the right call.

Chapter 12
Where is the Cure for Cancer?

Inspiration

"God is our refuge and strength and ever-present help when in trouble."

– Psalms 46:1

"There is always hope beyond what you see."

"I believe that God intends for us to turn our suffering into hope for the future."

"Control what you can control – your thoughts, your words, your actions, your attitude, your faith, and leave the rest to God."

Over 1.9 million people were newly diagnosed with cancer last year alone, and they join the 19 million currently fighting this horrible disease. We have all lost someone to cancer. I believe that most of us want to know why, after 100 years of research and billions of dollars spent looking for a cure, we don't have one. Are the cures being suppressed to continue making money? Are people dying because of greed? It sure looks that way. When you can come up with a COVID-19 vaccine in less than a year, it really makes you wonder.

So, I started learning more about cancer and why it is such a complicated disease. While cancer survivors have more than doubled over the last 40 years, the odds of finding a single cure remain slim and may probably never happen. Cancer is not one disease. It is an umbrella term for more than 100+ diseases. Cancer cells within a tumor are not always identical, so while the treatment may kill most of the cells, a few may still survive.

I do believe that a cure will be found, as it says in 2 Peter, "His divine power has given us everything we need for life." I would love to see an American President put together a group of the best scientists from around the globe and come up with a cure—do it right in front of Big Pharma's face. Plus, working closely with other countries might build relationships between nations. Lord knows we need that.

Sorry if I digressed, but I have seen far too many incredibly young people bravely fighting this terrible disease.

Chapter 13
Mayo Clinic Referral

Inspiration

"There are wounds that never show on the body that are deeper and more hurtful than anything that bleeds."

– Laurell K. Hamilton

"Remember that hope is the last thing ever lost."

– Robin Age

"Believing that tomorrow will be better, we can face tough times today."

"It is not what we choose that is important. It is the reason that we choose it."

– Caroline Myss

Well, at this point, I am unable to eat and rely entirely on a PEG tube for nutrition. I can't talk, and I'm forced to communicate using a small greaseboard. (Later, we found a small electronic board that allowed me to write with my finger, then simply press a button to erase everything—a small but helpful improvement.) I choke very often, even on fluids, and I'm struggling to maintain weight. To make matters worse, my original reconstruction doctor was no longer available.

Gina has not fully recovered emotionally from how long the coma dragged on, especially once we discovered it had been drug-induced.

Gina and I both felt an urgency to move things forward, knowing that time was not on our side. She asked Dr. Pinheiro if he could help us get a referral to Mayo Clinic.

Fortunately, Dr. Pinheiro was friends with Dr. Moore, an extremely talented ENT at Mayo. I don't fully recall how the two physicians originally connected, but Dr. Moore had ties to Missouri and had known Dr. Pinheiro for quite some time. A simple phone call between them was all it took. Dr. Moore agreed to take me on as his patient, and my medical records were sent over for his review.

I was genuinely excited about this opportunity to work with Mayo's physicians. They are among the very best in the world, and the level of professionalism, pride, and care—not just among the doctors but throughout the entire organization—was truly remarkable. Next stop: Dr. Moore.

Mayo has clinics in Minnesota, Florida and Arizona. The largest and original location is in Rochester, Minnesota, which is where I would receive my care.

From our home, Rochester was about a 9 to 9.5-hour drive, essentially a full day's journey each way. With treatments scheduled, each trip easily turned into a full week away from home. Little did I know at the time that I would make many such trips.

Dr. Moore was everything I hoped for: a true professional and a highly skilled ENT. He accepted me as his patient and recommended that we attempt another flap rebuild surgery. So, once again, we were preparing for yet another procedure.

The surgery appeared to go well at first. However, after about two days of healing, the team became concerned about the color of the flap. While the skin itself looked promising, the bone placed in my throat showed troubling signs—the same issue that had plagued my previous surgeries. A second surgery was quickly scheduled to try to save the bone.

So, we waited anxiously for a few more days. The medical staff came in multiple times daily, checking the color, monitoring the site, and even trying to make the tissue bleed to assess viability. But despite their efforts, it became clear that the flap was failing. A third surgery was scheduled—this time for flap removal. Once again, we lost ground.

Now, I was being sent home to recover and heal. The plan was to return in eight weeks to reassess and determine the next step.

Mentally, I was deeply discouraged. But one thing I quickly learned was the critical role of a positive mental state in the healing process. Staying optimistic, even in the darkest moments, became essential for my recovery. You'll read much more about that in the "Lessons Learned" chapter.

For now, my condition remained unchanged. I had a hole in the palate area of my mouth. With a hole there, sound can't project properly—like shouting into a cave, where your voice simply dissipates. I couldn't eat or swallow fluids; everything—liquids and nutrients—had to go through the PEG tube. I still required significant help just to get through daily life.

At this point, I had undergone nine surgeries, and I was still in bad shape. I could barely talk (relying mostly on the grease board to communicate), could barely swallow, and choked easily. Eating was nearly impossible. Heavy use of protein drinks was keeping me alive. I desperately needed God's help now more than ever. My wife began putting together a prayer chain.

Chapter 14
Is There Something
Wrong with Me?

Inspiration

"Everybody has been touched by cancer in one way or another. Be kind – everybody is healing from something."

"Sometimes you have to have faith, even when you don't understand."

"Faith is hope when all else seems lost."

– Catherine Pulsifer

"If you are afraid, do it afraid."

– Joyce Meyer

After an 8-week healing period, I returned to Dr. Moore. He recommended that I meet with Mayo's Dental Specialties group, as they could build an obturator to cover the hole, help my voice project outward, and improve my ability to swallow. I took his advice, and we scheduled an appointment with them.

The repeated failures were beginning to take a heavy toll—not only physically but mentally and emotionally as well. I never lost my faith, but something still felt off. Was I the problem? Was there something inside me that was causing all these failures? It certainly felt like something was preventing the bone from healing properly, and it weighed heavily on my mind.

Every time they moved both bone and tissue, the tissue managed to heal, but the bone continued to struggle for survival. With each failed attempt, the weight of it all grew heavier. I couldn't shake the unsettling feeling that something was wrong with me—something beyond what the doctors could see or explain. The thought gnawed at me, almost to the point where I feared taking the next step. I had already climbed to a higher level of care, working with some of the best doctors available, yet the difficulties persisted. Still, I held on to my faith, leaned even harder into prayer, and tried to summon the strength to keep moving forward, one step at a time.

Chapter 15
Next Stop Dental Specialties

Inspiration

"Let your hopes, not your hurts, shape your future."

– Robert Schuller

"Every failure is another step closer to winning. Never stop trying."

– Robert M. Hensel

"No matter what has happened to you in the past or what is happening right now, walk by faith in God."

– Joyce Meyer

"Pray, be generous to others, get inspired and surround yourself with people that you admire."

At this point, I had a larger hole in the palate area of my mouth. Three attempts to close the hole had failed due to the bone portion of the flap not surviving after being moved.

So now I was headed to Mayo's Dental Specialties Group. Dr. Salinas directed this group, and they were highly skilled at rebuilding the mouth and throat area.

The plan at Dental Specialties was to build an obturator (in Latin, *obturator* means "to close a hole"). The obturator being built would serve two purposes. First, it would cover the hole in the roof of my mouth, fitting snugly inside and capping the opening. Then, the device would extend downward into an upper denture.

A good amount of work went into building the Obturator. If I remember correctly, it took about two to three weeks to get it sized properly and functioning inside my mouth.

Once the Obturator was complete and finally working, keeping it securely in place was always a challenge. It was bulky and had a slight heaviness to it. Since there was no bone in the palate area, there was only soft tissue for it to attach to. Keeping it securely in place was always difficult.

However, it did help with my voice projection. It also allowed me to eat some soft foods, which I hadn't been able to do in nearly two years. I still had a stomach tube, and most of my nutrition continued to go through it.

Weight loss was always a major concern for my wife, Gina. Being an RN, she knew that weight loss was often an indication of how well I was doing in my overall recovery. My battle to maintain weight through all of this remained a constant struggle.

I stayed in this state for a few months. This was probably the point where I should have said "enough" and stopped. I believe that if, at the time, we had found a way to secure the obturator, so I could have spoken a little better and eaten a little better, I would have stopped there. It's hindsight now, but I think my wife and I both feel the same way.

On one of my routine visits to Dental Specialties, I happened to ask Dr. Salinas if he knew anyone who might be able to help me. He smiled and said, "I sure do." He mentioned Dr. Mardini, who was head of the Plastic Services Division at Mayo. Right then, Dr. Salinas picked up the phone and called Dr. Mardini's office to see if he was available. It happened to be a surgery day for Dr. Mardini and his staff, but due to a cancellation, he was in between surgeries and happened to be in the office.

Dr. Salinas was so kind. I found it incredible that he would walk me over and personally introduce me to Dr. Mardini. It's things like this—personal care and attention—that make Mayo Clinic such a special place. Dr. Salinas went out of his way, personally walked me over, and introduced me. Before we left, he also contacted Dr. Mardini's nurse resident, gave her my patient number, and had my health record pulled up in advance.

After the introduction, Dr. Mardini spent a good amount of time examining me and reviewing my patient record. He said he could help me and welcomed me as a patient.

Chapter 16
Dr. Samir Mardini

Inspiration

"Why do we close our eyes when we pray, cry, kiss or dream? Because the most beautiful things in life are not seen but felt by the heart."

– Denzel Washington

"My faith helps me understand that circumstances don't dictate my happiness or my inner peace."

– Denzel Washington (my favorite actor)

"Courage isn't having the strength to go on, it is going on when you don't have the strength."

– Napoleon Bonaparte

"Two things in life that define you: Your patience when you have nothing and your attitude when you have everything."

– Jason Luke

I still to this day think that Dr. Mardini was Godsent. He is one of the best Microfacial Surgeons in the country. He is Chair of Plastics and Reconstructive Surgery and is the Director of Face Transplants at the Mayo Clinic. Dr. Mardini has a passion for helping others. He brings hope, compassion, intensity and dedication to his patients. He performed Mayo's first-ever successful face transplant and gave new life to a patient who definitely needed it. In his passion to help others, he has traveled the world helping both children and adults who need cleft lip and palate repair.

I would hate to think where I would be without Dr. Mardini. Dr. Mardini realized that my body did not tolerate the movement of the bone (why that was a problem, we may never know). So, two things were discussed with Dr. Mardini. The first was building my palate with soft tissue layers, and the second thing that we discussed was getting me into oxygen therapy to help with my healing. My wife and I liked both ideas, and that is the direction we headed.

I believe the surgery was completed right before Christmas in 2017. The soft tissue procedure was successful, and we were able to finally close the hole finally. I was in the hospital for a couple of weeks after that surgery. Then I was released to start oxygen therapy.

I will end up having several more surgeries with Dr. Mardini, so we will be back to discuss this more.

Chapter 17
Oh, The Children

Inspiration

"Pray, be generous to others, surround yourself with people you admire."

"Listen more to God and less to your doubts. You will be on the right path."

"Sometimes it just takes a little kindness from one hurting soul to another to change us forever."

– Karen Kestyla

"BELIEVE. Believe you can win. Believe in yourself. Believe you will survive. Believe that God has given you everything you need; he will direct your steps and supply your needs."

So, for the next several weeks, I went in Oxygen Therapy (to improve my healing). I needed a place to stay since I would be there for an extended time. Most decent motels start at $100 a night and go up from there, so finding a place to stay for an extended period was not just important—it was absolutely essential. That's why I feel incredibly grateful for the American Cancer Society and its beautiful two-story building in Rochester called Hope Lodge. The lodge, which takes up nearly an entire city block, stands as a beacon of hope for people like me who are fighting cancer. They offered me a room completely free of charge, lifting an enormous burden off my shoulders during one of the hardest times of my life. Knowing I had a safe and welcoming place to stay gave me the comfort and peace of mind I desperately needed. Thank you, Hope Lodge, for being there when it mattered most.

Hope Lodge was filled with so many beautiful people, both old and young, each carrying their own stories and battles. Despite their different backgrounds and journeys, they shared one powerful thing in common: they were all courageously fighting the same horrible disease called cancer. At Hope Lodge, the rooms were large (maybe a bit larger than most hotel rooms). The rooms were nice and comfortable. Up to two family members could stay alongside the patients, which meant no one had to face such a difficult time alone.

One of the things that made Hope Lodge so special was its three very large kitchens (if I remember correctly), where people would gather each evening. In these kitchens, every patient had their own set of cabinets and shared a refrigerator with two other tenants. It created not just a place to cook, but a place where connections blossomed. After long, draining days of treatment, people came together in the kitchen and dining areas, preparing meals, sharing stories, and finding comfort in one another's presence. It became a warm and welcoming hub for building friendships and finding strength. There were people there from many different states and even different countries (Japan, Korea, Taiwan, UK), all there for the same purpose and united by the same challenges. There was an unspoken bond among us, a shared understanding that transcended language and culture, and it made Hope Lodge feel like a true community, bound by hope and resilience.

Dinner time was when we all truly got to know one another and spent meaningful time together. Several local organizations, businesses, and churches generously provided evening meals for everyone at Hope Lodge, and through them, we met so many wonderful people who dedicated their time and kindness to lifting our spirits. Sometimes, groups would come in to play instruments, sing, dance, and provide entertainment, filling the lodge with music, laughter, and moments of escape from our worries.

As we grew closer to the guests at Hope Lodge, I was especially struck by how many children were there, bravely fighting cancer. Cancer does not discriminate by age—there were children, teenagers, young adults, and older adults all facing the same cruel disease. Yet in the midst of it all, they prayed for one another and cheered each other on. Hope Lodge is truly a heart-touching place, and it's hard to put into words how deeply it affects you.

During my stay, it was the small children who especially touched my heart. As an adult, hearing the words "you have cancer" is devastating, but to be told your child has cancer must be unimaginable. Trying to make sense of such a situation has to be mentally and emotionally exhausting. We've all seen those St. Jude's and Shriner's commercials showing beautiful children with infectious smiles, but living alongside these families brought it closer than any commercial ever could. I believe it was something God wanted me to see. In the eyes of these children, I saw pure beauty and innocence. Their smiles were truly infectious and carried a light that could brighten even the darkest days.

Despite the enormous challenges they faced, you often couldn't tell it by the smiles on their faces. Some of these children endured months and months of treatment. Their whole world revolves around hospitals, clinics, labs, and places like Hope Lodge. One thing that has always fascinated me is how many children were encouraged to draw pictures expressing their feelings. It was incredible to see how some of them were able to pour out their emotions through art. Many of their drawings hung throughout Hope Lodge, adding color and hope to the hallways.

My heart went out to those children, and being among them truly grounded me. It reminded me just how fortunate we are when our kids and grandkids are healthy.

Hope Lodge didn't have televisions in the rooms, but they did have an extensive collection of movies and several "viewing rooms" with large screens where guests could watch films. I found a small movie room tucked into one of the building's corners and used it often because it was usually quiet and empty. Then one day, an 18-year-old young man named David began using the room as well. David and I struck up a friendship. He was from Ohio, and shortly after graduating from high school, he was diagnosed with a brain tumor. He'd come to Mayo Clinic for treatment, with his mother staying by his side, while his father visited on weekends whenever he could. David loved sports and had been a baseball player, so we found plenty to talk about.

One day, I stopped by the viewing room to check on David, and he seemed to be struggling. He couldn't get the movie started and appeared confused, as though he was having trouble thinking clearly. I helped him set up the movie, but I could see that he couldn't focus. As I tried making conversation, something unexpected and heartbreaking happened. David looked at me with a puzzled expression and asked softly, "Are you my dad?"

After a brief pause, I gently replied, "No, David, we're just friends. Sometimes we visit and watch movies together."

It was clear David was really struggling, and it broke my heart to see how quickly his condition seemed to have worsened. I quietly stepped out and went to find his mother. She came and took David with her, and I never saw him again. It was truly heartbreaking.

Hope Lodge was filled with moments of hope and joy, as well as moments of deep sadness and struggle. Hope Lodge and the incredible people in it have truly touched my soul, and I believe it was a place God wanted me to experience.

Chapter 18
The Oxygen Experience

Inspirational

"Thank God for each day, recognizing it is a precious gift."

"Let the uncertainties and challenges that you face pull you closer to God."

"Tough times never last, but tough people do"

– Robert H. Schuller

"Although the world is full of suffering, it is also full of overcoming it."

– Helen Keller

Your body's tissues need an adequate supply of oxygen to function properly. When tissue is injured, it requires even more oxygen to survive. During my earlier procedures, where they moved bone, tissue and veins, the procedure kept failing, and I had tried several times in an attempt to do this successfully. Each time it failed.

When Dr. Mardini began working on my palate rebuild, he explained that there was a good chance my tissue needed more oxygen to survive. It was then recommended that I try Hyperbaric Oxygen Therapy, so that became our next step.

Hyperbaric oxygen therapy increases the amount of oxygen that your blood can carry. With repeated treatments, these higher oxygen levels help promote normal tissue growth—and that was precisely what we had hoped to achieve. Hyperbaric oxygen therapy involves breathing pure oxygen in a pressurized environment. It's especially helpful for wounds that are having difficulty healing due to diabetes or radiation injury. In my case, we believed my case was radiation injury from the large doses of radiation that I had previously received.

Inside a Hyperbaric Oxygen Chamber, the air pressure is two to three times higher than normal atmospheric pressure. This allows your lungs to gather much more oxygen, which improves healing. I always felt fantastic after leaving the oxygen chamber. That extra oxygen truly made me feel energized and well. It's a relatively safe procedure, though I sometimes experienced pressure in my inner ear—a very common side effect. However, the nurses and staff at Mayo Hyperbaric were excellent about checking everyone's ears before and after treatment, and my ear pain usually subsided once the pressure equalized.

There are two main types of Oxygen Chambers. One is a single-person unit where you lie down on a table that slides into a clear plastic chamber. Staff can watch you through the chamber walls to ensure you're doing well under pressure. There is a television just outside the unit, so you can watch TV if you like. Alternatively, you can sleep or read during the procedure, which lasts about two hours.

Mayo Clinic also has one of the largest oxygen chambers in the world and has provided over 30,000 therapies. I believe the chamber can accommodate up to 16 patients, along with two nurses who are there to assist anyone who experiences issues during the procedure. The nurses monitor you throughout the treatment. Most patients (who are not in wheelchairs) sit in lounge chairs that can recline, lie flat, or remain upright. One of the main differences between the large chamber and the single chamber is that in the large chamber, you receive your oxygen through a clear hood, which is worn throughout

55

the full procedure. There is one break where you can remove the hood for a short time.

I underwent oxygen treatments during three separate periods. The longest session that I had was after palate reconstruction surgery and consisted of 40 treatments. There were two additional rounds of treatments after other surgeries, but those were much shorter. Still, I enjoyed the treatments and loved how great I felt afterward.

The therapy team does a great job of checking every patient after each treatment. They check your ears, blood pressure, pulse, and listen to your heart and breathing. If you have diabetes, they also check your blood glucose levels and get you ready for discharge.

I would like to acknowledge the entire healthcare team at Mayo Hyperbaric. From the doctors to the nurses to the entire staff, they are some of the most professional people I have ever encountered. Their care is exceptional, and they put an enormous amount of pride and dedication into their work. They are true professionals. They even came in on a holiday to give me treatment. I enjoyed working with them and truly valued the experience.

Chapter 19
Now That Sucks

Inspiration

"Believe in yourself. You are braver than you think, more talented than you know and capable of more than you can imagine.

"Never underestimate the power of little victories. Take one step at a time."

"Be grateful. A grateful heart is a magnet for miracles."

"Keep smiling. Your smile makes life more beautiful."

In my case, blood flow after the Flap Surgery (where they move tissue, bone and veins) was always an issue in my healing. The problem consistently involved the bone. The surrounding tissue seemed to survive just fine, but the bone was either failing or teetering on the brink. Keeping the bone alive became a challenge that my doctors struggled with repeatedly.

When I finally reached Dr. Mardini, he suspected that blood flow to the bone might be the weak link that needed addressing. And soon enough, we found out he was exactly right.

We started with Oxygen Therapy, then discussed using a "double-barreled" approach that included trying leech therapy. Let me be clear—this was purely optional. It was a newer treatment at Mayo where they use leeches (yes, those little bloodsuckers found in lakes and streams) to increase blood flow in targeted areas. These creatures can dramatically improve circulation to specific parts of the body.

I was willing to try anything that might improve my chances of staying alive and getting healthier. At first, I didn't really think through what it would mean to have leeches used so close to my throat. It only dawned on me later that this would involve putting them inside my mouth. Wow… talk about being clueless.

I didn't end up having many treatments because the staff quickly discovered that, in my case, it wasn't an easy process. They did everything they could to protect me, even building a barrier so I wouldn't accidentally swallow one of the little critters. Let me tell you—keeping my head in the right place for this took some serious mental gymnastics (and yes, I'm laughing even as I write this).

We had only tried this about four or five times when I had an issue. One of the interns managed to drop one down my throat, forgetting to put the barrier in place.

The poor intern was visibly shaken and, without a word, bolted from the room. I had no idea where she was going, though I assumed she was off to get help. Sure enough, a few minutes later, the entire ICU team came streaming into my room. There were three doctors, my nurse, the head of Biomed, the head of Radiology, a representative from Respiratory, someone from Cardiology, and probably a few others I'm forgetting.

They quickly set up an X-ray unit with a scope and ran it down into my stomach. And there it was: the little creature, now staring at the monitor. One of the biggest concerns was whether the leech might have ended up in my lungs—but thankfully, it was just in my stomach (thank God for small mercies).

At that point, the entire medical team huddled together, debating whether they should sedate me and go in to retrieve the leech. You have to understand—this was a first for everyone. Even the excellent

ICU team at Mayo hadn't encountered this situation before. And to make matters worse, my throat was already sore from surgery, and now they were talking about running scopes back down it.

Then one of the doctors spoke up and said, "Just leave it."

He explained that the leech would simply pass through my digestive system and come out in my bowels. So that's what they decided: wait and see. The staff kept a close eye on me for the rest of the day.

That evening, I finally had a bowel movement—and sure enough, out came the leech. I'd bet it was one of the most witnessed bowel movements in Mayo history (and yes, I'm laughing about it now).

I can laugh at myself, and I can laugh about what happened—but let me assure you, there was nothing funny about it at the time. I kept asking myself: how the heck did I get myself into this mess? There are a few parts of this whole battle that I'd love a do-over on—and this incident sits right at the top of that list.

As far as I know, I was only the second patient at Mayo who'd ever tried leech therapy. And after my experience, I might just have been the last (and yes, I'm laughing again).

Chapter 20
Christmas and the Storm

Inspiration

"Be thankful for the bad things in life. They open your eyes to the good things you were missing."

"Be strong. You never know who you are inspiring."

"Be strong but not rude. Be kind but not weak. Be humble but not timid. Be proud but not arrogant."

– Jim Rohn

"There is no reward without work, no victory without effort, no battle won without risk."

– Nora Roberts

In 2019, about 2 weeks before Christmas, I underwent one of the biggest surgeries of my life. It was an extremely serious surgery and lasted several hours. This surgery involved another big flap move. I will say that not everything went smoothly during the surgery, and, like some of the previous surgeries, healing the bone that had been moved became an issue.

A lot of work was done, and I wound up in the hospital (both ICU and a Nursing floor) for well over two weeks. My stay overlapped Christmas, and I was still in the hospital, trying to recover from everything. Gina made a couple of trips back and forth and ended up spending Christmas with me in the hospital. We hated missing

Christmas with the kids and grandkids, especially the little ones, since Christmas is always a fun time with them. We wound up telling our family that we would have our own Christmas celebration when we got home. We told them to focus on God and their own families, and we would have our own celebration when we could.

Gina and I spent Christmas alone in a hospital room. It was never any fun, but we made the most of it. I think that it was the first time that Gina had been away from her family for Christmas. In my case, I had spent some Christmases in Germany during my Air Force days.

I was eventually discharged from the hospital. We were able to do some celebrating with family, although I was still in rough shape.

On the day I was discharged from St. Mary's Hospital, we started what would turn out to be an unimaginable trip back home. On that day, a blizzard with heavy snow and strong winds hit the Midwest. It extended from Minnesota all the way to Arkansas, and we were right on that path.

As we crossed Iowa, the wind was strong, visibility was poor, and the snow was blowing laterally across the traffic lanes. It was a long, slow drive, and Gina drove the entire way herself, as I was not able to drive. She was on pins and needles the whole drive, but the determination and stamina that she showed during that monstrous trip were amazing. Gina had never driven in a storm before, and this was the mother of all storms— what an experience!. She was a Trooper that night and my hero.

We probably should have found a motel somewhere and gotten to a much safer place, but instead, we kept trudging through the storm as Gina needed to be back to work. She had taken FMLA just to be with me through this huge surgery, and she was due back at work and extremely concerned about missing any more time, so we kept going.

That is one drive that Gina and I will never forget. While road crews were trying to keep the snow cleared, I must believe that the snow might have been winning that battle.

One thing that played in our favor that night was the vehicle that we were driving. I owned an H-3 Hummer that I absolutely enjoyed driving. I have kept the Hummer longer than any vehicle that I have ever owned. It is awesome in snow and very slick conditions; it has both all-wheel drive and 4-wheel drive. I can't think of another vehicle that I would have rather been in that night.

The weather was not the only thing that was bad that night, as I began having an issue with the Flap area that I had just had surgery on. We slowly crossed Minnesota and about 90% of Iowa when the new flap area of my throat started bleeding. The surgery that I had was an attempt to close a hole in my throat. We were on Interstate 35 and reached a community named Van Wert, Iowa (about 21 miles north of the Missouri state line), when I started bleeding. Gina had so much pressure on her just driving through the storm; the last thing she needed was me bleeding. She is a Registered Nurse, and she knew that I could lose the flap, so now Gina was starting to panic even more.

Then she got on her cell phone, called our oldest daughter, Heather and asked her to search for a hospital near where we were. Heather found a hospital in Osceola, Iowa, which was about 10 to 15 miles in our rearview mirror. So, in the middle of this blizzard, we turned around and backtracked to Osceola, Iowa. We found the hospital; it was small and had an emergency room, which was open. By the time we reached the hospital, I had put enough pressure on the bleeding area that the bleeding had stopped.

We were sitting outside in the ER parking area, but had not entered the ER. I wasn't feeling good about this, and I needed to decide whether to enter or just go on. My gut feeling was not good about entering the hospital.

At this point, I needed to mention the blue-eyed wolf, and I have a full chapter near the end of this book telling the story and its significance. Native Americans believe the wolf to be a spiritual pathfinder that can come into your life when you are at a crossroads of decision. This wolf kept returning in my dreams.

Once again, I needed to decide which path to take, and my pathfinder, the blue-eyed wolf, was in the back of my mind, reminding me to be true to myself in my decision. I prayed about it and decided not to go to the ER. This flap surgery was very expensive (probably about 6 figures), and the last thing I needed was to have a small-town General MD messing with it. No disrespect to small-town doctors— and they probably would have referred me to a hospital where more specialists were available. But in that situation, I still wanted the best care that I could get. Besides, the bleeding had stopped. It was a risk that I was taking, a big risk, but I felt good about the decision.

I discussed it with Gina, who was nervous now, and told her that I wanted to travel on towards Kansas City. If I had any further issues, we could head for one of the big hospitals like KU Medical Center or St. Luke's. The decision had some risk as we were probably still 130+ miles away and probably traveling 35 to 40 miles per hour.

The decision turned out to be a good one, and when we finally reached Kansas City, there had been no more bleeding, and the Flap seemed much better. So once again, I found myself at a major crossroads. The decision now was whether to stop at KU or move on. Yes, that blue-eyed wolf was still in the back of my mind, encouraging me to decide and stay true to myself. Gina and I discussed it, I prayed, and the decision to move on was made.

We eventually got home, safe and tired. It was about 2 a.m. Gina had to get up and go to work at 5 a.m. and only managed to get about three hours of sleep. Still, we survived the whole ordeal, and yes, my Flap survived. As I mentioned earlier, Gina was a trooper. She was the real warrior here. I must express my admiration for her and all I put her through. I am glad that I had her along with me.

Chapter 21
Trusting God in Difficult Times

Inspiration

"Because you are a survivor of the unfairness of life, you are stronger than you think and more capable of achieving far more than you believe."

– Zero Dean

"Be a warrior and work through whatever that life throws your way with courage, love and positivity, and continually push forward".

– Zero Dean

"Don't compare your life to others, you have no idea what their journey is all about".

– Regina Brett

"If we threw our problems in a pile and saw everyone else's, we would grab ours back".

– Regina Brett

Many of us have a vision of what we want our lives to look like. We have plans, goals, and dreams. Then suddenly, something happens— something bad, something challenging, something that we were not expecting. Something that makes us wonder, "What are we to do next?"

How do we trust God when going through difficult times? How do we have faith when our world falls apart and a sense of disappointment grips our hearts? You feel stuck in a place that you don't want to be. You also struggle to understand how this could be God's plan for you?

We may never know why God allows us to go through tough times. It is important to understand that everyone in the Bible went through difficult times, and we will too. Combine that with sins destructive impact on the world, and life can be unfair and full of challenges. God uses the darkest moments as a training ground for building your faith and drawing you closer to Him. Still, even in our darkest moments, God is working to bring beauty to our situation.

Jesus warned us that in this world, you will encounter challenges. When there are no challenges in life, trusting God is easy. But we grow the most spiritually during our struggles. Trusting God during tough times requires faith and prayer. Faith does not make things easy; it makes them possible. Your pain has a purpose, even when you don't understand why. Every challenge that you face is preparing you to be stronger and pulling you closer to God.

I am going to end this chapter with a quote from Ralph Waldo Emerson.

This is My Wish for You

Comfort on difficult days, smiles when sadness intrudes, rainbows to follow the clouds, laughter to kiss your lips, sunsets to warm your heart, hugs when spirits sag, beauty for your eyes to see, friendships to brighten your being, faith so you can believe, confidence for when you doubt, courage to know yourself, patience to accept the truth, love to complete your life.

Ralph Waldo Emerson

Chapter 22
Blue-eyed Wolf

Inspiration

"The chances that you take, the people that you meet, the people that you love, the faith that you have. That is what is going to define you."

– Denzel Washington

"The easiest thing to be in the world is you. The most difficult thing to be is what other people want you to be."

– Leo Buscaglia

"You may say that I am a dreamer, but I am not the only one. I hope someday that you will join us, and the world will live as one." Quote from a John Lennon song.

"When it hurts to look back and you are scared to look ahead, you can look beside you and God will be there."

I started the book with a story about wolves, and now I am going to end it with one. I talked with God throughout this battle, which seemed never-ending. I know it says in the Bible, "that God will never give you more than you can endure," but I must admit that I thought that I was two or three steps over that line.

Through it all, my battle included 9 total years, 25 surgeries, 3 trips to the Mayo Hyperbaric Chamber, a 6-week stay at Hope Lodge (Mayo's Cancer Residence), numerous doctors, numerous trips to

Rochester, Minnesota and a huge depletion of our funds. Yet I NEVER LOST FAITH.

While my wife, children, and close family tell me that I am one of the toughest men they've ever met, I was just trying to survive. Besides, I hope there is more to my legacy than toughness. Through it all, I needed God more than ever, and I kept my faith, which I have detailed throughout this book.

Back to the wolf. What does a wolf (especially one with blue eyes) have to do with my cancer fight? For the longest time, I didn't know myself. Yet, I kept dreaming about this wolf.

Right after Christmas 2022, I entered Mayo for what was supposed to be my last surgery. Nine months earlier, I had undergone a surgery called a Flap, where they move tissue (bone, skin, muscle and veins) from one area of your body to another. This surgery took a toll on three things: my face, my back and my pride. So, this surgery was to debulk the Flap. I was in the hospital after surgery for about 10 days. Normally, when I am in the hospital, I read, watch television, listen to music, do a quick Facebook check and rest. This time, I decided to do something different and spend time in silence with God.

In the last couple of years of my journey, I had at least 5 or 6 dreams, where I was out in the woods and was being watched over by a wolf. It was always a comfortable feeling when the wolf appeared. In some of the later wolf dreams, the wolf got closer to me and always seemed to be watching over me. I had never had dreams like that, where I had the same dream over and over. This seemed very strange to me.

I felt like Kevin Costner in the movie "Dances with Wolves". In one of the dreams, the wolf got very close, and I could see that it had blue eyes, which got me thinking about the fact that my mother had blue eyes and passed them down to her children.

Now it was something that I started to pay more attention to and give more thought to, especially since it was recurring. I rarely have dreams, and not recurring. Did this dream represent my mother looking over me with beautiful blue eyes? My mother died the same month that I was diagnosed.

Since this dream kept recurring, I wondered: was there a message in the wolf, or was it just a dream? I started becoming more curious. Back during my hospital stay, I finally ended the silence (between hospital staff interruptions, as I laugh), and turned on the television. I must laugh when I said that one of the movies on television was "Dances with Wolves." This all seemed to be more than a coincidence at this point. Was there a message here? It has my attention. So, I watched *Dances with Wolves,* this time with more focus on the wolves.

After the movie, I had even more curiosity, so I started studying the traits of wolves to learn more about the one that kept appearing in my life (I laughed again).

I wanted to see if there was some sort of common identity or message, perhaps even a place in this healing/recovery process. Surprisingly, I found some reflection and some spirituality in that search.

Many Native Americans tribes believe that wolves are "spiritual pathfinders," and when they appear, they are there to help you realize yourself and gain your full potential. They commonly appear when you are at a "decision crossroads" in your life. Wow— I had to make so many decisions over the cancer years, and still had more decisions to make during all this reconstruction. While my family has some

Native American blood, I don't think that anyone ever checked to see how much. My father was raised in Quapaw, Oklahoma, among several members of the Quapaw Indian Tribe, so there is a strong relationship to the Native Americans, even if there is no strong bloodline.

I examined the traits of the wolf, and they really resonated with me. Here is what I found:

- Physically strong

- Mentally strong

- Natural leaders

- Dedicated and protective of family and pack. The wolf only mates once, but continues to look over its family its whole life. Especially the elders.

- Freedom

- Independence

- Connection to nature

- Intelligence

I think that I checked off all the boxes. Additionally, living life with a purpose has always fostered strong individuals, and this is a notable trait of wolves.

Wolves are believed to be <u>spiritual guides to the afterlife</u> in many cultures in Europe and North America. In the Celtic countries, wolves were guardians and protectors of the forest. In many cultures, wolves are revered as noble warriors, great leaders, and protectors of the innocent.

I also found that having "blue eyes" is believed to offer protection against bad luck. It's also said to ward off negativity that may come my way.

I am a *fan of the Yellowstone TV series, and in Season 4, I recall Kayce frequently encounter*ing a wolf. As he searched for a message, he eventually asked the Spiritual Leaders. The Spiritual Leaders placed him in a small outdoor enclosure (like a very small horse corral) where he had to remain until he had an answer. Like me, Kayce was at a decisional crossroads and was battling to choose between two paths.

So, what was my wolf telling me? My wolf was telling me that I was at a crossroads on a couple of decisions. One of those was whether or not to continue the surgery. Most people could not do what I had done; most people could not go through half of what I had been through. I had physically put my mind and body through so much. The wolf was telling me to connect more with my inner being, to trust my intuition, my intelligence, my instincts and my gut feeling. I needed to choose a path with courage and determination. At that point, I decided to walk away. I had beaten cancer; I had won the battle. I was still somewhat handicapped, but thankful. Thank you, Jesus. While I am not sure where the wolf came from, I am thankful there too.

Chapter 23
25 and Counting

Inspiration

"Sometimes it is more about the journey than the destination."

– Jamal Crawford

"Look back in forgiveness and always look forward in hope."

– Zig Ziglar

"Success is the ability to go from failure to failure without losing enthusiasm."

– Winston Churchill

At this point, I have had 25 surgeries. I had put my body and my mind through so much in hopes of getting some normalcy in my life. My face is scarred, my ego bruised, and all the effort, pain, and suffering that I had gone through have taken me to a better physical state, but have fallen short of my expectations. I am alive and thankful for that. I can live with the scars.

I am still challenged in a couple of areas, mainly speech and eating. The speech and eating issues are something that I will address down the road. I am currently discussing those issues with Dr. Mardini, and he thinks that with minor surgery, we can help with those issues. We will see. Right now, I am considering this the end of my journey.

The 51 Lessons that I Learned Fighting Cancer

Cancer has not run much in my family, so when it struck, I was surprised. I believe that sharing your experiences and emotions is beneficial, especially if it can help others. Besides, it is not the things that you do for yourself, but the things that you do for others that become your legacy. Sharing might help the next fighter, and that is one reason that I felt compelled to write this. I tried to learn as much as I could from the experience, as you should always learn from your challenges. So, I made a list, and if it helps even just one person fight this tough disease, then the time that I spent writing this was worth it.

1. **Double team this**. Pray as if everything depends on God, fight as if everything depends on you.

2. **Your approach is important**. Approach your disease with strong faith, optimism and remarkable grace. Approach is the beginning– yes, it is important.

3. **Self-Belief**. You are braver than you think, more talented than you know and capable of more than you can imagine. Self-awareness is very important. Check it daily.

4. **Bow your head**. The most important message here is that you need God in your corner to help you beat cancer. If you don't know God, I suggest that you please bow your head and pray (start talking to him).

5. **Successful people have boundaries**. Never let success get to your head or failure get to your heart. Important not only in your battle with cancer but in your everyday life.

6. **Strength in numbers**. Never underestimate the power of God or the power of prayer, especially in large groups. Unleash an army of people to pray for you. There is strength in numbers.

7. **Best medicine**. Always remember that prayer is its own type of medicine. Try several doses daily.

8. **Pull God closer**. During the darkest times, always pull God closer to you. Enough said, turn it over to him. Where else can you turn for help?

9. **Right state of mind**. The mind is one of the most powerful tools in your fight against cancer. A huge part of the battle is getting yourself in the right state of mind, as your mind needs to make you stronger and lift you up. <u>Remember, successful people win the battle in their minds.</u>

10. **Positive mindset**. Never underestimate the power of a positive mindset. A positive mindset can be our greatest ally, and it is not just a catchphrase. A positive mindset can change the way we perceive our own capabilities; it is truly about embracing optimism and believing in our abilities to succeed. It can lead to positive achievements. <u>Our life is what our thoughts make it.</u>

11. **Mind, body, spirit**. There is a connection between mind, body, and spirit. I firmly believe that a positive mindset helps both your body and spirit, as they are all tied together. <u>Think like you are blessed, talk like you are blessed, fight like you are blessed, and act like you are blessed. Your body and spirit are listening.</u>

12. **Power of Positivity**. Positive thinking is a valuable tool that can help you overcome obstacles, deal with pain and reach new goals. Positive thinking can boost your immune system,

reduce stress levels, reduce the risk of cognitive decline and improve your mental health. It is time to experience the power of positivity; it may change your life.

13. **Don't fight cancer lying down.** I believe this to be a huge step in your battle to fight cancer. This is a mental step and a conditioning of the mind. Sit up, stand up, walk if you are able. You are conditioning the mind and saying, "that you are not going to take this lying down." Cancer, radiation, and chemo will zap your strength. Please sit up if you can, and I repeat, "don't fight cancer lying down."

14. **Negative thoughts in healing**. Negative thoughts or emotions counteract positive healing. Don't waste your time on anger, regret, worries, or grudges. They all affect the body and hinder healing. Not many things can help people with the wrong mental attitude. Again, keep your thoughts positive.

15. **Surround yourself with people who are going to lift you up**. A strong support network of people is huge in your fight, and so is the outpouring of love. You need family and friends who encourage you, cheer you on and stand by you. No naysayers allowed. When someone truly loves you, they give you support unconditionally and without hesitation. Loyalty is everything.

16. **Replace fear with faith**. Fear is the enemy; it is persistent and will become a big part of your journey. It will steal your thoughts, emotions, and influence your decisions. When you focus on faith and your ability to overcome, you can succeed. Replace fear with faith.

17. **Your time to conquer fear**. You can conquer almost any fear if you just make up your mind to do so. Remember that fear does not exist anywhere but in your mind. Step outside your

comfort zone and discover the sensuality of fear. <u>Every day, someone must conquer fear – now it is your time.</u>

18. **Be grateful**. <u>A grateful heart is a magnet for miracles.</u> Always have an "attitude of gratitude." If the only prayer that you ever say in your lifetime is "thank you," that is a great start.

19. **Find your courage**. Find courage, stay calm, grow your bravery, as cancer is a tough fight. <u>"An important note here— courage is often found in your quiet moments with no audience."</u> Time to dig deep within yourself. You can do this.

20. **Don't be afraid**. Easy to say, not so easy to do. The one statement that God made more than any other statement in the Bible is, "Don't be afraid."

21. **Never lose hope**. Hope must be the last thing ever lost. <u>Remember, there is always hope beyond what you see.</u> Only when it is dark enough can you see the stars.

22. **Your reaction**. Life is a small part of what happens to us and a very large part of how we react to it. Courage, toughness, confidence, patience, resilience, perseverance and faith are good reactions. <u>Make failure something to build on and learn from.</u>

23. **Attitude is so important**. Everything that we do can be affected by our attitudes. Attitude is a choice and one of the most important in our lives. A change in attitude can cause drastic changes in your healing and your life. <u>Attitude determines your actions, and actions determine success.</u>

24. **Cancer will try to define you**. The girth of the pain that you feel is physical, emotional and spiritual. Pain and challenges have a way of defining us, stealing our dignity and self-worth.

You are not defined by what you are going through. <u>Stop beating yourself up, as you are a work in progress.</u> Success is how you carry yourself every day.

25. **Your comfort zone**. Step outside your comfort zone. Success and comfort do not always co-exist. Most people choose a comfort zone of less struggle, less fighting and less pain. The last thing that you need. In your fight, you will learn that your comfort zone is not always that comfortable. <u>Comfort may be an enemy</u>.

26. **Inner strength**. Stay positive and be the strong person that God intended you to be. True strength is when you have so much to cry for, but instead, you smile. <u>The difference between success and failure can be just a little more effort and a little more strength. True faith fuels inner strength.</u>

27. **Learn and grow**. Overcoming cancer or any other life-threatening disease should always have a positive effect on the rest of your life. Hopefully, it will make you smarter, stronger, kinder, more flexible, more loving, more thoughtful, more appreciative and more thankful.

28. **Expect ups and downs**. You will encounter obstacles and have ups and downs in your fight with cancer. Don't be discouraged, stay determined, choose to be courageous. You may have failed, but you are not a failure until you give up. <u>You will gain strength, courage and confidence by staring fear in the face.</u>

29. **Quit overthinking**. An enormous problem in your cancer battle is the amount of overthinking that you do. Quit overthinking things. Overthinking makes you worry, and it makes your challenges seem worse. <u>Make peace of mind one of your highest goals</u>.

30. **No Laziness**. There is no laziness in healing. Time, energy and sacrifice are very important ingredients. There should be no complacency. <u>Success is never accidental. Keep working.</u>

31. **Your calm mind is a weapon against cancer**. Finding a state of calmness in this battle is very important. Calmness causes you not to overreact to your challenge. It keeps your mind clear and your heart at peace. A calm mind is a big weapon against all life challenges. <u>Also, the more confident and tranquil your mind becomes, the better your chances for success.</u>

32. **Recognize small victories**. Never underestimate the power of little victories, as they are significant and can fuel motivation and inspire you. Take one step at a time, as healing is a marathon, not a sprint. <u>Success does not happen overnight.</u>

33. **Peace of Mind discipline**. Remember to control your thoughts; becoming the best version of yourself requires discipline and mind training. Train your mind to be stronger than your emotions. <u>Don't let worrying steal your peace of mind</u>. A disciplined mind can create self-control, determination and motivation. <u>Peace of mind is vital to success.</u>

34. **Cancer is a tough disease**. <u>You must be tougher than it is</u>. Tough times don't last, but tough people do. Life's challenges should always make you tougher and wiser. Toughness is a mindset and commitment. <u>A huge part of toughness is keeping faith through your biggest challenges.</u>

35. **Cancer is a determined disease**. <u>Cancer is a determined disease, and you must be more determined than it is.</u> When I hired people, I liked the "D" words (drive, desire, dedication,

dependability, discipline and determination). They can all help you at work and in most of your life challenges.

36. **Embrace unconditional love.** As part of conditioning the mind, always remember that unconditional love is a stimulant to the immune system and one of the best gifts that you can give to yourself. <u>Know your self-worth.</u> Wrap yourself up in unconditional love.

37. **Cancer hates hugs and kisses.** Hugs and kisses represent more than affection, as they represent safety and security at a time when your mind and heart need both. Pull your loved one close.

38. **Share love and kindness.** Your inner strength shines brightest during times of kindness and compassion. If you share love and kindness with people when fighting your toughest battles, that is what you will get in return.

39. **Forgive.** One of the biggest threats to healing is the inability to forgive. Even The Lord's Prayer mentions to forgive twice. <u>Forgiveness frees you from your past, and your focus needs to be forward</u>. Forgiveness heals the heart and soul. Forgive yourself and forgive others.

40. **Adjust your priorities**. A battle with cancer will show you your many blessings. Your family, your friends and your relationships will all have greater importance. Life is short; adjust your priorities.

41. **The price of success in anything is discipline**. Discipline is a rare commodity in our pampered society, but it is enormous in your battle with cancer. Discipline is needed to achieve anything of significance in life. It takes discipline to show physical, mental and spiritual improvement, and all three are

part of the beat cancer mindset. <u>Mental discipline is about doing what is right when it is hard, when you are stressed and when everything inside you says quit.</u>

42. **Learned deep-controlled breathing**. It is great for the mind; Also good for the body, and it controls the nerves. <u>Breathe your anxiety away</u>.

43. **Laughter is its own medicine**. Make sure you laugh, as it is also good for the mind and body. It is tough to laugh while fighting cancer, but do it anyway. It is also one of the best medicines for relieving stress. It also enhances respiration and improves circulation. Laughing is good for the heart; smiling is good for the soul.

44. **Music is its own type of medicine**. It relaxes the mind. Music can help you cope with emotion. Music is a divine way to tell beautiful things to the heart. Music touches people when words cannot. <u>Let it relax you</u>.

45. **Read cancer survivor stories**. They are good for the mind and show you hope. They also show you that you are not alone. You just read my story, and I won against incredible odds.

46. **Self-talk**. Self-talk is more important than we realize. Encourage yourself, discipline yourself, push yourself, coach yourself, and motivate yourself. Nobody talks to you more than you.

47. **Always remember to be persistent in prayer**. There is no wrong way to pray; Do it in church, home, or outdoors. Do it in silence or out loud, alone or with others. I used to imagine God riding in the empty passenger seat of my car, and I would talk to him. I think that counts too.

48. **Focus on all three**. Your mind, your body and your spirit. Don't forget spirituality in this battle. It helps you see things from a bigger perspective and fosters inner peace. It helps you control emotions and stress. It can alleviate anxiety and depression. It can form close bonds with family and friends. Scientific power will not outperform spiritual power.

49. **Say thank you daily**. Thank God daily, for each day is a blessing and a realization of just how precious life is. I know, as I have seen how easily it can be taken away.

50. **Envision yourself**. Envision yourself as healthy, cancer-free, blessed and happy. Envision success. Keep looking forward. Make plans for tomorrow and plans for your future, as that is a part of the beat cancer mindset.

51. **Believe.** Turn doubt into belief. When you believe in yourself, beautiful things can happen. When you have no confidence, you are already half defeated, so believing with confidence can get you halfway there.

Believe you can get well and survive. Believe God is with you every step of the way. Believe that you were made for something bigger.

Closing

Inspiration (Finishing with a few kindness quotes)

"Everybody can use some kindness in their life; kindness starts with you."

"We change the world by one act of kindness at a time."

– Morgan Freeman

"There is no such thing as a small act of kindness."

– Author unknown

"Kindness begins with the understanding that we all struggle."

– Charles Glassman

"Too often we underestimate the power of a touch, a smile, a kind word, a listening ear, an honest compliment, or the smallest act of kindness, all of which have the potential to turn a life around."

– Leo Buscaglia

Somewhere I read that life begins at the end of your comfort zone – I now understand that. In your comfort zone, most people choose a path of less struggle, less fighting and less pain and those three paths are the last thing that you need in a cancer fight. Success is found in discomfort and hard work.

The life that you had before cancer is over, gone, and you can't get it back. You can't continue looking back. You must move forward, and it is important to believe that your future will be better than your past.

It is important to understand that you are not always in control. Life is full of surprises and sometimes full of pain, heartbreak, and challenges. Life is also full of overcoming all those things. Life is also full of lessons, and it is important to learn from all these challenges.

Setbacks only defeat you if you quit. When you get knocked off course, and it will happen, just point yourself back in the right direction, keep moving forward, but never quit. No matter what your circumstances, do not give up on yourself. Show up for yourself and battle every day. Tough people don't stay down; they always get back up. Toughness is a choice, a mindset, and a commitment. Tough people may show hurt, they may even cry, but they never quit.

Take one day at a time, one step at a time and never underestimate the power of little victories. Do what you can and let God handle the rest. I repeat: "Pray as if everything depends on God. Fight as if everything depends on you." In the Bible, it says, "For I will restore health unto you, and I will heal you of your wounds, says the lord" – Jeremiah 30:17. Just believe.

Always stand with faith, a pure heart, a great mindset, and an understanding that you have a purpose. There is always a lesson to be learned. Ask yourself, what is this challenge or this pain trying to teach me?

Alone time is important as it is where you find your most courage, where you find time to reflect, build, and strengthen yourself. Be silent, listen to your heart and passion. Find some alone time daily.

Having a healthy mind is key to your overall health. A healthy mind influences how you make decisions and handle stress. Emotionally healthy people are typically in control of their thoughts, feelings, emotions, and actions. They cope with life's challenges and heal quickly from setbacks.

As we go through our many circumstances in life, you can become a victim of those circumstances or a survivor. Choose to survive and become a better version of yourself than you were. There is always room for improvement. The challenges that you face should always make you smarter, stronger and more flexible. They should also make you kinder and more loving.

There is an old saying about the word impossible. It is missing an apostrophe and a space – I'm possible. Believe in yourself, you are braver and more capable than you can imagine.

If I could talk to my younger self, I would say this: "Challenges build character and help you know who you really are. You will never reach your potential until you challenge yourself." I would also say, "Step away from this busy world and do self-examination." Ask where you are going with your life, examine your decisions, your values, and most importantly, ask yourself, "Are you living with a purpose?"

Another thing that I learned in my many battles is that the more confident and tranquil a person becomes, the better the odds for their success. Rather, it is poise or confidence, and I see it as important. I also learned the importance of pausing. Pause, step away from it all, breathe deeply and pray. Do it several times a day.

In closing, remember there are things that cancer cannot do. Cancer cannot destroy love, take away hope, take away your faith, silence courage or kill friendships.

A Few Notes to My Grandchildren and the Parents Trying to Raise Them in the Cell Phone High-Tech Information Age.

While I managed to read several books over the years (and hopefully you will too— put down those phones), I never imagined myself writing one. But here I am, maybe it was God's will. So, while I have your attention, I have a few messages of hope for you. Before I begin with the messages of hope, however, I have one message for your parents.

To the parents: Cody, Alyson, Melissa, Heather, Jesse, Kainon, Amber

Some of my concerns are about managing children with a constant cell phone in their hands. First, excessive screen time affects their homework, their physical activity, their sleep patterns, and I firmly believe it also affects their cognitive development. It causes social isolation when they need to be learning face-to-face social interactions with family and friends. I worry that age-appropriate filters are not in place, and discussions about appropriate internet usage are probably not taking place. Besides inappropriate content, there are strangers who may be predators, bullying, and possible dangerous interactions in their and your privacy. Too much screen time can cause addiction, and the media will straight face lie to get a point across. So please be engaged in your child's digital life, have rules, check in from time to time to see who they are engaging with and regularly have open discussions about what they are doing online. It is bad now, and going to get worse, so good luck managing that. You are doing a good job raising the children, so keep that up. We are proud of them.

Grandchildren: Kaia, McKinzie, Acacia, Sydney, Elias, Lilly and Azayla, with greats Emiliah and Calihan: Here are some things I hope:

I hope that you have challenges, tough times, and disappointments in your life.

You see, overcoming challenges, tough times, and disappointments builds character, builds confidence, teaches you who you are, makes you appreciate life even more and helps you explore the spiritual side of life.

I also hope you have success and happiness. Although I hope the success and happiness that you experience do not come easy. I hope that you receive it through hard work and dedication.

I hope you understand just how much your parents and grandparents love you, even while you are being punished. There is something to learn from each punishment, and it means that you are loved.

I hope that your parents, coaches and teachers mentally push you, challenge you, demand the best from you and chew you out if they must. It means that they want the best for you, they want to see you succeed, and it means that they are invested in you.

I hope that you stand up and fight for the things that you believe in even if you get a bloody nose or skinned up legs.

I hope that you see enough hatred and ugliest in the world that you grow a big heart and grow even bigger values.

I hope that you get embarrassed enough that you learn humility.

I hope that you get beaten enough that you learn true sportsmanship.

I hope that you learn that being good at anything requires hard work and dedication.

I hope that you see enough less fortunate people in the world that you learn how fortunate that you are.

I hope that you see enough unkindness in the world that you learn to be kind.

I hope that you see enough disrespect in the world that you learn respect.

I hope that you see enough self-centered people that you learn to be respectful, unselfish, grateful, kind and helpful.

I could go on and on, but instead, I am going to throw one more out there that worries me. I hope that you are never bullied and that you never bully anyone. I hope that you learn to show sympathy and humility to anyone being picked on. You never know what challenges they are going through in their lives.

A huge problem in the world today is that it is always creating and magnifying disparities such as race, age, financial differences and religious beliefs. It's time for your generation to recognize and stop that.

Last, I hope that you learn that one of the most beautiful things that you can say to someone is "thank you." Please say it to God daily.

You are all beautiful, and you changed my life without even trying, and I don't think that I could ever tell you just how much you mean to me.

Love always,

Papa.

End Note

I am not a writer. I am a reader and a student of life's challenges and life's many lessons. My cancer battle (which started in the palate area of my throat, even though I was a non-tobacco user) covered 9 years, 25 surgeries, and 16 days in a coma, where I stared death in the face. My journey also included 1 year being unable to speak, 2 years being unable to eat (my nutrition came through a PEG tube). I encountered surgery failure after surgery failure after surgery failure.

My face was disfigured, and I had scars from my face down to my ankles. I spent a small fortune on doctors, surgeries and medical care. Yet through it all, I never lost my faith, never lost hope, never lost confidence in winning my battle.

Through it all, I learned many lessons. Lessons about who I was as a person, lessons about my faith, my determination and my values. I also learned 51 lessons about fighting cancer. I learned that the cancer battle was about so much more than doctors, surgeries, radiation and chemo. I learned that cancer fights are also about mind, body and spirit. I tried to capture that in this book. I am also a "Cancer Survivor" and my cancer journey was unique and took me to some unique places, practices and experiences. It was not a stay-at-home journey. So, I also managed to tell my own story of cancer survival.

Most importantly, the reason for writing this book was the 51 Lessons that I learned and wanted to share with other people, in hopes it might help someone fight cancer.

My wife kept encouraging me to write this, and after a lot of prayer, I felt like God wanted me to share my message.

www.ingramcontent.com/pod-product-compliance
Lightning Source LLC
Chambersburg PA
CBHW051326120626
46547CB00015B/2414